I Get Energy from the Sun

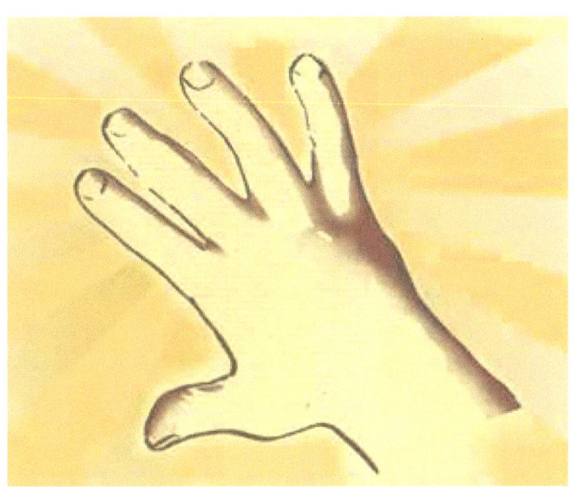

by: Kajara Nia Nebthet
Illustrated by: Jacqueline Thompson

I dedicate this book to Black and Brown children all over the world.
May we all find our way home.

— *Kajara Nia Nebthet*

I have energy within me.

I have energy wheels within me too.

They are called **aritu or chakras.**

I get good energy from eating fruits and vegetables.

I get good energy from laughing,

I recharge my energy when I am sleeping.

Rekhit Kajara Nia Yaa Nebthet an author, healer, priestess, teacher, artist and founder of the Ra Sekhi Arts Temple. She has dedicated her life to heal and uplift people by promoting health and wellness in the community. She has been teaching children of all ages for over twenty years. She loves working with children.

She is available for classes, consultations and presentations.
Visit: www.rasekhihealing.com and www.rasekhistore.com
Email: rasekhitemple@gmail.com

Jacqueline Thompson is a resident of Asheville, North Carolina, graduated from the Corcoran College of Art in 1984 with a degree in Graphic Design. As a graphic designer and web developer, she enjoys working with non-profits, teaching art and creative writing to children.
See more of her work at:
Website: jmmthompson23.dunked.com
Email: jthompson2329@gmail.com